D1212956

EXPLORING THE OCEAN DEPTHS
The Final Frontier

PETER JEDICKE

A+

PHOTO CREDITS

Page 4: courtesy NASA. Page 5: courtesy Peter Parks/imagequest3d.com. Page 8: courtesy Fotosearch LLC. Page 9 clockwise: courtesy Geoff Tompkinson/Photo Researchers, Inc. Courtesy Steve Fisher. Page 10: courtesy of OAR/National Undersea Research Program (NURP), University of Connecticut. Page 11: courtesy National Oceanic and Atmospheric Administration (NOAA)/Department of Commerce. Page 12: courtesy NOAA/Department of Commerce. Page 13: courtesy OAR/NURP. Page 14: Art by Joe Bailey, after pry.com/smog/bath_detail.html. Page 15: courtesy NURP, Harbor Branch Oceanographic Inst. Page 16: courtesy NURP, Woods Hole Oceanographic Inst. Page 17: courtesy OAR/NURP, Rutgers Univ. Page 18: courtesy of and copyright © 2003 RMS Titanic, Inc. Page 19: ISE Research Ltd. Page 20: courtesy Todd Walsh copyright © 2001 MBARI. Page 21: Art by Joe Bailey, after Extremscience.com. Page 22: U.S. Department of the Interior, U.S. Geological Survey. Page 23: courtesy NOAA/Department of Commerce. Page 24: courtesy Dr. Ignacio Pujana, Geosciences UTD. Page 25: Art by Joe Bailey, after www.world-builders.org and Elizabeth Anne Viau. Page 26: courtesy Paul H. Yancey, Whitman College, Walla Walla WA. Page 27: copyright © 2003 Ablestock collection. Page 28-29: copyright © 2003 Dr. Neil Sullivan, University of Southern California. Page 30 top and bottom: courtesy NURP, University of South Carolina; Courtesy NURP. Page 32: courtesy NASA. Page 33: courtesy Paul H. Yancey, Whitman College, Walla Walla, WA. Page 34-35: Copyright © 2003 Harbor Branch Oceanographic. Page 36: courtesy John Sullivan and Monica Rua of Ribbit Photography. Page 37: courtesy OAR/NURP, NOAA. Page 38: courtesy B. Murton/Southampton Oceanography Centre/Photo Researchers, Inc. Page 39: courtesy OAR/NU. Page 40: courtesy NASA. Page 42: courtesy OAR/NURP, Sea Technology. Page 43: courtesy OAR/NURP. Page 44: Copyright © 2003 F. Jack Jackson. Page 45: Art by Joe Bailey, after Jonathan Newman. (And a special heartfelt "Thank You!" to Photo Researchers, Inc).

Published by Smart Apple Media
1980 Lookout Drive, North Mankato, Minnesota 56003

Produced by Byron Preiss Visual Publications, Inc.

Copyright © 2003 Byron Preiss Visual Publications
Printed in the United States of America

Edited by Howard Zimmerman
Associate editor: Janine Rosado
Design templates by Tom Draper Studio
Cover and interior layouts by Gilda Hannah
Cover art: Courtesy NOAA

Library of Congress Cataloging-in-Publication Data

Jedicke, Peter.
Exploring the ocean depths: the final frontier / by Peter Jedicke.
p. cm. — (Hot science)
Summary: A discussion of the oceans and oceanography, the science of the sea.

ISBN 1-58340-367-1

1. Oceanography—Juvenile literature. [1. Oceanography. 2. Ocean.] I. Title. II. Series.
GC21.5.J43 2003   551.46—dc21   2003041643

First Edition

9 8 7 6 5 4 3 2 1

Without ever leaving the surface of Earth, a person who travels a few miles or kilometers straight down below the ocean waves will arrive in another world. This is less than the typical distance between two exits along a highway, yet it is a trip most human beings can make only in their imaginations. So close, yet so hard to reach, the ocean depths of Earth have even been called "inner space" and "Earth's final frontier."

Human beings have always gone out to sea with great enthusiasm. The sea promises a more immediate reward than outer space. There are rich resources, such as oil and minerals, not too far away. Most people will have a greater chance to

Opposite page: **More than two-thirds of Earth is covered by water, as can be seen in this beautiful image of the planet shot by an Apollo astronaut.**

Right: **The Portuguese man-of-war is a jellyfish and a colony creature. Its tentacles are actually composed of groups of individual creatures. Its sting can paralyze and kill even humans.**

work and live in the ocean than to fly into space. Is there an Atlantis in the future, even if there never was one in the past?

The science of the sea is called "oceanography." Imagine how different the map of the world would look if the water were not drawn in! One would see that the seafloor below the oceans has mountains, plains, and even rivers that don't appear on a globe or world map. The total amount of land under the oceans is more than *double* the land area outside the oceans—a little more than two-thirds of Earth is covered with water. The oceans even have a kind of weather; about the only thing missing is clouds.

And there's life down there in the inky depths, where sunlight does not penetrate. It is a strange and eerie sort of life that looks and feels as alien as anything anyone could ever imagine. Some of the creatures look fearsome; others are just weird. Think of a jellyfish, a Portuguese man-of-war, for example—has there ever been a creature so alien-looking in a science-fiction movie?

Finally, the oceans are the key to our origins. Life began in the oceans. To explore the oceans is to explore ourselves, what we are and where we came from. *Exploring the Ocean Depths* goes there.

Undersea Potential

"The discoveries beneficial to mankind will far outweigh those of the space program over the next couple of decades. If we can get to the abyss regularly, there will be immediate payoffs." (Bruce Robison, Monterey Bay Aquarium Research Institute, 1995, commenting on the potential for developing the untapped resources of the ocean depths.)

Down into the Sea

CHAPTER ONE

When people swim below the surface of the ocean for a few seconds, water surrounds them completely. They hold their breath, but not because there's no oxygen in the water; there is simply no mechanism in the human body to collect the oxygen molecules from the water, the way fish do through their gills. Oxygen molecules—which are composed of two oxygen atoms held tightly together—easily dissolve in water when storms or ocean waves stir up the sea. The oceans need oxygen to support undersea life just as the oxygen in Earth's atmosphere supports life on land. Cold water holds more oxygen than warm water, so the polar seas are the best place to recharge the oceans' oxygen supply. Cold water is also heavier than warm water. So the recharged water sinks and flows around the world on the bottom of the oceans.

Another important characteristic of the oceans—especially for deep-sea explorers—is pressure. Pressure is caused by the weight of water, which is about 62.4 pounds per cubic foot (1,000 kg per cu m). Pressure is a measurement that tells how a force, such as a push, is spread out over a surface, such as the skin of a swimmer. When swimmers go underwater, the weight of the water above them presses all over their bodies. We are used to having air pressure around us all the time, and we don't notice most changes in air pressure. A basketball, for example, has the same pressure of air on the inside as on the outside. The two pressures balance, and the basketball holds its shape.

But water is almost 1,000 times heavier than air, so water pressure is extremely powerful. If someone wanted to take a basketball 3,300 feet (1,000 m) underwater, he would have to pump it up so much that every 15 square inches (100 sq cm) of the basketball could support a push of more than 10 tons (9 t)! Of course, the

same pressure would also squeeze a person to pulp. Twice as deep would mean twice as much pressure, and so on.

A person may think that water is clear when holding a glass of it. But water does absorb light. Going down 66 feet (20 m) underwater is enough to cut out 99 percent of the sunlight shining on the surface. Descend 10 times farther than that, and a dim, bluish gloom is all that remains of the Sun's light. Below about 1,600 feet (500 m), no ray of light can penetrate at all. From this depth on down to the seafloor, there is perpetual darkness.

The temperature of the oceans varies much less than that of the air and the land. Water has an amazing heat capacity—it takes a lot of energy to change the temperature of water. Sunlight warms the ocean layer at the surface, and the water mixes up and down so that the temperature changes only 10 to 20 degrees down to a depth of

Humans cannot swim underwater for too long, nor can they dive too deeply, since they cannot draw oxygen directly from seawater as fish can, nor can they withstand the pressure of the water below a few dozen feet (12 m). Because of these facts, most of the ocean depths remained unexplored until quite recently. They continue to be Earth's last frontier.

about 500 feet (150 m). Summery seas can be as warm as 100°F (38°C).

Another characteristic of ocean water is its salinity, or saltiness. Polar seas are a few percent less salty because ice that melts in those regions is made of fresh water. Water just a few percent more salty lies in the warmer, tropical regions north and south of the equator. This slight difference actually can be noticed by human beings. Animals that live in the sea have salty blood, or they could not tolerate the salinity. Humans also have salty blood, another sign of our oceanic origins. Salt is made of the chemical elements chlorine and sodium, and these are the most common elements found in seawater. Dozens of other elements are present in tiny proportions. There are even 2.2 pounds (1 kg) of gold in every 220,000 tons (200,000 t) of seawater!

Oceanographers use specialized words to describe different aspects of the ocean. The water itself—all of it—is the "pelagic zone." Anything near the bottom, whether under shallow or deep water, is called the "benthic zone." The vast deep areas are referred to as the abyss, or the "abyssal zone," and the very deepest individual places are the "hadal zones." Each of Earth's major

Top: An Atlantic jack swims in near-surface waters. This species, and many other species of fish and jellyfish, spend most of their lives in the life-friendly pelagic zone.

Bottom: Life also exists on the ocean bottom. Down there, where no light penetrates the eternal gloom, creatures do not have much color. In this picture, a ghostly spider crab is eating tube worms.

More examples of life on the ocean floor. A portunid crab pauses at the base of a sea anemone called *Cerianthus borealis*. The light source is the photographer's camera.

What's in the Water?

A block of ocean that measures 3,300 feet (1,000 m) on each side contains 2.2 trillion pounds (1 trillion kg) of water. There would also be the following:

MAJOR ELEMENTS	(TONS)	(METRIC TONS)
Magnesium	1,390,000	1,272,000
Sulfur	972,000	884,000
Calcium	440,000	400,000
Potassium	418,000	380,000

MINOR ELEMENTS	(TONS)	(METRIC TONS)
Bromine	72,000	65,000
Carbon	33,800	28,000
Strontium	14,300	13,000
Boron	5,100	4,600
Silicon (no more than …)	4,400	4,000
Fluorine	1,600	1,400

Trace Elements: At least 30 others, including manganese, copper, zinc, lead, silver, vanadium, nickel, gold, radium, and tin.

landmasses has a continental shelf around it, where the ocean is not as deep as it is farther away from the land. But the deep areas dominate the planet: 80 percent of the ocean is more than 10,000 feet (3,000 m) deep. Oceanographers have calculated that the average depth of all the oceans is 12,566 feet (3,831 m).

Voyages of Discovery

A human cannot swim more than 30 to 40 feet (9–12 m) underwater without special gear. But for thousands of years, human beings have lived by the sea and roamed across its surface. The ancient Phoenicians crisscrossed the eastern Mediterranean and were excellent navigators. This was at a time when "exploring the ocean" meant finding out what the land was on the other side of it. Christopher Columbus and Ferdinand Magellan are two well-known explorers who remained safely above the waves.

An obvious way to learn about what was *in* the sea was to lower a rope down. In 1840, Sir James Ross of the British Royal Navy ship *HMS Erebus* used this technique, called "sounding," to make the first accurate depth measurement of 14,550 feet (4,436 m) off the coast of Antarctica. Lines with grabbing attachments were used to bring back material from the bottom. Sir John Ross, who was James Ross's uncle, brought worms and mud up from a depth of 6,000 feet (1,800 m). This proved that there was life down there. Serious exploration began with the three-year voyage of the *HMS Challenger* that started in December 1872. The *Challenger* was a true research vessel that sailed around the world and expanded scientific knowledge of the sea and the life in it.

An old engraving shows the crew of the *HMS Erebus* (seen in the background) taking soundings to determine the depth of the ocean. You can see one of the crewmen actually lowering the rope off the stern of one of the small boats.

H.M.S. "Challenger."

An engraving of the _HMS Challenger_, a research vessel that actually sailed around the world in 1872. It took a strong, courageous, and dedicated crew to complete this voyage of exploration.

The idea of slipping under the water in a sealed vessel must have occurred to many inventors before Cornelius Van Drebbel, a Danish doctor, built an underwater rowboat in 1620. Then, in 1690, astronomer Edmund Halley designed a bell-shaped platform that could be lowered down and supplied with air through tubes. Another example of a sealed vessel was the submarine _Turtle_, invented by David Bushnell at the beginning of the American Revolutionary War. It was made of wood and was intended to sneak up on—and ram headfirst into—warships at anchor. But no ships were ever sunk by the _Turtle_. None of these early efforts ever descended much farther down than 15 feet (4.5 m) below the surface.

Although submarine technology improved greatly, submarines early in the 20th century were used exclusively in war. They were not designed to go down farther than 820 feet (250 m). It was Otis Barton, an engineer, and William Beebe, a naturalist and author, who built the first apparatus designed purely to send a human being deep into the ocean. They called it a "bathysphere." Less than five feet (1.5 m) across, it was built of steel, with three small windows and a hatch that had to be bolted shut.

Lowered over the side of a ship on the end of a thick cable, with a second cable for electricity and telephone, the 4,500-pound (2,050 kg) bathysphere carried Barton and Beebe down to a record depth of 3,028 feet (923 m) near Bermuda in 1934. If the cable had snapped, the bathysphere could not have made it back to the surface on its own. Barton then set another record in 1949 when he made a dive to 4,500 feet (1,372 m) off the coast of California in a slightly larger sphere he called a Benthoscope.

French balloonists Auguste and Jacques Piccard, father and son, took the final leap in deep-sea discovery with the invention of the "bathyscaph." The word means "deep boat," and, unlike the bathysphere, the motion of the bathyscaph could be controlled by the crew. The sphere that contained the crew hung under a large tank filled with gasoline, which made the ship buoyant, or able to rise in the water. Naming his deep boat the *Trieste I*, Auguste Piccard set one depth record after another in the 1950s. Then came the fateful day when human beings reached the bottom of the world. On January 23, 1960, Jacques Piccard and Don Walsh, a U.S. Navy officer, settled with a gentle thump on the bottom of the Marianas Trench in the western Pacific Ocean. At 35,800 feet (10,911 m), this is the deepest spot ever found in the oceans.

No human being has ever been that deep again. The *Trieste I* made many dives before being retired. These included a photography mission to the *USS Thresher*, a nuclear submarine that had imploded in 1963. The wreck was lying on the bottom of the Atlantic under 8,400 feet (2,560 m) of water. There have been many important deep-sea

The *Turtle*, a Revolutionary War submarine, was human-powered. It also had no way of renewing its air supply, which made its voyages short—or deadly. This was not a successful design.

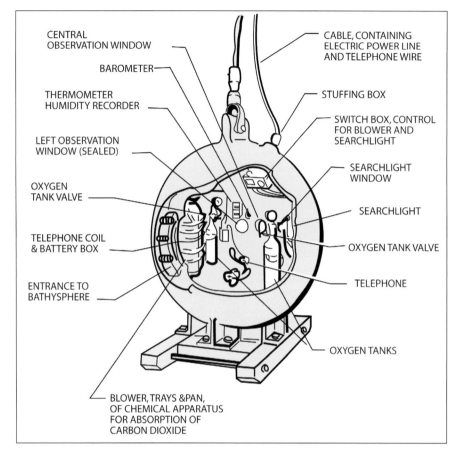

CENTRAL
OBSERVATION WINDOW

BAROMETER

THERMOMETER
HUMIDITY RECORDER

LEFT OBSERVATION
WINDOW (SEALED)

OXYGEN
TANK VALVE

TELEPHONE COIL
& BATTERY BOX

ENTRANCE TO
BATHYSPHERE

CABLE, CONTAINING
ELECTRIC POWER LINE
AND TELEPHONE WIRE

STUFFING BOX

SWITCH BOX, CONTROL
FOR BLOWER AND
SEARCHLIGHT

SEARCHLIGHT
WINDOW

SEARCHLIGHT

OXYGEN TANK VALVE

TELEPHONE

OXYGEN TANKS

BLOWER, TRAYS & PAN,
OF CHEMICAL APPARATUS
FOR ABSORPTION OF
CARBON DIOXIDE

A cutaway view of the bathysphere Otis Barton and William Beebe used to set the record for the deepest ocean descent by humans. It was quite cramped.

salvage operations, especially for the military. Another famous incident involved the recovery by *Trieste II* of a lost nuclear weapon in the Mediterranean Sea in 1966. One of the ships used in that adventure was *Alvin*, the most successful undersea vessel ever launched. *Alvin*, *Trieste*, and other ships like them are called "submersibles," meaning that they operate underwater, to distinguish them from "submarines," which can function either underwater or on the surface.

The crew compartment of *Alvin* is six feet (1.8 m) across. For flotation, *Alvin*'s upper hull contains millions of tiny air-filled glass beads instead of gasoline. Its shape is angular and a bit clunky; this vessel was not built for speed. The fastest it can go is about half a mile (800 m) per hour. In the exciting decades of *Alvin*'s service, it even suffered the misfortune of sinking once. Fortunately, the vehicle's pilot was able to escape before it sank too deep, and *Alvin* was hauled back to safety a couple months later. By the year 2003, *Alvin* had made almost 4,000 successful dives. The maximum depth that *Alvin* can reach is just about 14,800 feet (4,500 m). There is currently no submersible that can descend to the deepest points in the hadal zones.

Active Submersibles

SUBMERSIBLE	COUNTRY	MAXIMUM DEPTH	ENTERED SERVICE
Johnson Sea-Link I/II	United States	9,900 feet (3,000 m)	1971/1975
Cyana	France	9,900 feet (3,000 m)	1969
Alvin	United States	14,800 feet (4,500 m)	1964
Mir I/II	Russia	19,700 feet (6,000 m)	1987
Nautile	France	19,700 feet (6,000 m)	1984
Shinkai	Japan	21,300 feet (6,500 m)	1989

The _Johnson Sea-Link_ is prepared for a dive. Note the pilots' knees visible on either side of the joystick controls, seen through the clear acrylic bubble.

Robot Explorers

CHAPTER THREE

A former U.S. Navy officer, geologist Robert Ballard has made more than 100 deep-ocean dives. Among them was an adventure aboard *Trieste* when there was a gasoline leak, and it took him and his crew six suspenseful hours to make it back to the surface. Ballard has also made many dives aboard *Alvin*. But in 1984, Ballard said, "You'll never see much in *Alvin*; manned submersibles are doomed."

Alongside an undersea biologist in *Alvin* one day, Ballard was looking out the window at the fabulous sea life just an arm's length away. When he turned to his companion, he

Opposite page: The *Alvin* in action, descending to its maximum depth of 14,800 feet (4,500 m). Although it looks like it's moving away, that's actually the front end coming toward you.

Right: The *Alvin* is prepared for sample-collection dives off the New Jersey coast. Notice the small viewing window and the remotely operated arm. The operator inside the *Alvin* can use the arm to collect interesting plants and animals from the ocean bottom and then place them in the sample containers that are attached to the front of the submersible, below the window.

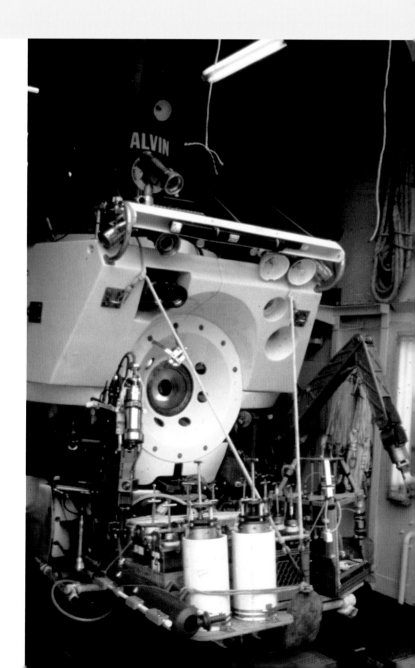

saw that the biologist was staring at the TV monitor, his back to the window. That's when Ballard knew the future would be in video cameras and remotely operated mechanical arms. Ballard calls technology his "passport to explore anything." He pioneered the use of "remotely operated vehicles," or ROVs.

The most famous dive by an ROV was made by Ballard's first remotely operated vehicle, the *Argo*. It was designed at the Woods Hole Oceanographic Institute, where Ballard has worked for 30 years. The *Argo* was a frame made of metal tubes, designed to be towed far underwater by a ship on the surface. *Argo* carried cameras that sent pictures up to the surface ship. In 1985, Ballard took *Argo* to the cold North Atlantic Ocean and found the wreck of the passenger liner *RMS Titanic* on the ocean bottom. The great ship had collided with an iceberg and sunk on her maiden voyage in 1912.

An actual photo of the sunken passenger liner *RMS Titanic*, taken from the *Alvin*.

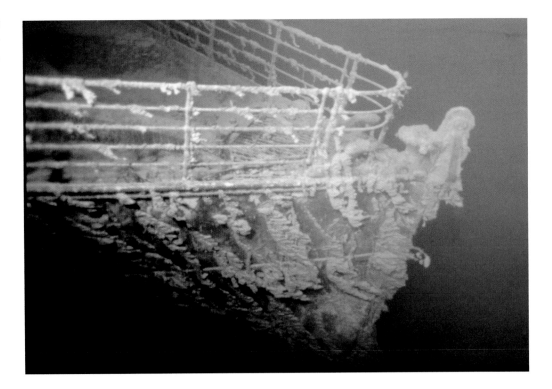

ROVs are tethered by cables to their mother ships and usually controlled from the surface. ROVs are built to float just above the ocean bottom, taking pictures and gathering data. They can be towed, like *Argo*, or outfitted with electric propellers for independent motion. Since a safe and reliable crew compartment is the most expensive part of a submersible, unmanned ROVs are a better value for getting scientific data or video footage. Many countries and oceanographic institutions operate ROVs. Some ROVs can dive to 19,700 feet (6,000 m) beneath the surface, and Japan's *Kaiko* can descend even deeper. *Kaiko* touched the bottom of the Marianas Trench in 1995—only the second time any ship has been there, more than 35,800 feet (10,911 m) down.

A robot vehicle that is autonomous, meaning that it is not connected to the surface ship by any cables, could also be used to explore the world under the sea. These machines are called AUVs, or "Autonomous Underwater Vehicles."

Autonomous underwater vehicles (AUVs) are shaped like torpedoes to cut smoothly through the water. This is the *Theseus*, developed jointly by the United States and Canada. In 1995 and 1996 it successfully laid long lengths of fiber optic cable below the Arctic ice pack.

The AUV *Dorado* being fitted for a deep-diving mission. It has modular components that can be changed out for different missions by removing the top half of the outer shell. The rear module (left) contains the propulsion and navigation units.

The maneuverability is even better than a tethered ROV. Barely past the experiment and testing stage, AUVs soon may be programmed and turned loose on their own for expeditions that last weeks or even months.

Another option for gathering information about the ocean is fixed stations with sensing equipment. To help weather experts predict the storm patterns known as El Niño, 70 buoys on the surface of the Pacific Ocean have been relaying data via satellite since the early 1990s. "Hydrophones," which are underwater microphones that can detect sound waves, have been installed in networks on the floor of both the Atlantic and Pacific Oceans to report on volcanoes and earthquakes. Many new projects make use of telephone or data cables that are lying on the seafloor but are no longer used by telephone companies or computer networks. From these projects we can expect a wealth of new physical information about the ocean in the near future.

Telepresence

Robert Ballard thinks that whoever is operating an undersea robot could be much farther away than the upper end of a tether. Why not send a live signal back to home base, or even to a museum? Then scientists could share the excitement of their discoveries with visitors and guests in real time. Ballard calls this "telepresence." A person at a museum might even be allowed to control a specialized robot over a telepresence link, guiding the robot through its underwater world.

The Ocean Floor

CHAPTER FOUR

The largest structures on Earth are tectonic plates. They are enormous pieces of Earth's outer crust. Thousands of miles in breadth, these immense rock slabs are only a few dozen miles thick. They are like cracked patches of eggshell on a hard-boiled egg. The tectonic plates, being on the outside, are cooler than the main body of Earth, called the "mantle." Earth's mantle is not only warmer, it is softer, and the tectonic plates slide over it. This motion has been carefully measured and has often been referred to as "continental drift" (even though each continent is not really on a separate plate, and some plates are entirely covered by the ocean). In most cases, the plates move just a few inches per year. But over millions of years, it adds up.

A subduction zone is created by an ocean plate being forced under a continental plate. Many times this kind of force will squeeze molten magma up from deeper in the earth and a volcano—or a string of volcanoes—will form on the surface.

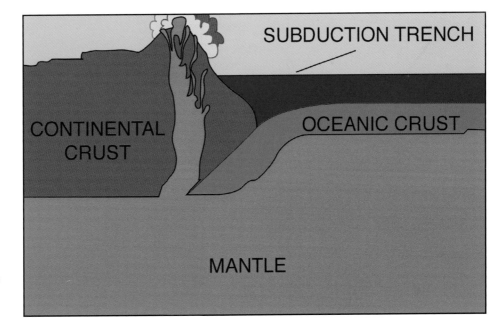

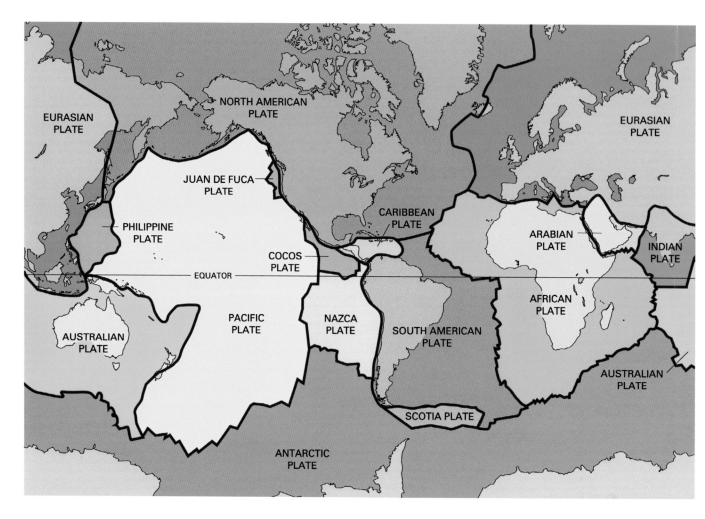

EURASIAN
PLATE

NORTH AMERICAN
PLATE

EURASIAN
PLATE

JUAN DE FUCA
PLATE

CARIBBEAN
PLATE

ARABIAN
PLATE

INDIAN
PLATE

PHILIPPINE
PLATE

COCOS
PLATE

EQUATOR

AFRICAN
PLATE

AUSTRALIAN
PLATE

PACIFIC
PLATE

NAZCA
PLATE

SOUTH AMERICAN
PLATE

AUSTRALIAN
PLATE

SCOTIA PLATE

ANTARCTIC
PLATE

A map of the earth without the oceans reveals the planet's tectonic plates. Where one plate pushes under another, mountains are formed.

Eight of the tectonic plates are larger than the others. But these don't match up well with the major landmasses of Earth's continents. Their higher parts are, indeed, the mountain ranges, basins, valleys, and great plains where human beings live. Almost all of the United States and Canada are part of the North American Plate. The highest place on land, Mt. Everest in Asia, is more than 29,000 feet (8,800 m) tall, but it is not the tallest mountain on Earth. That honor belongs to Mauna Kea, in Hawaii, which slopes down from the mighty summit, where telescopes peer into the night sky, right past the seashore and far under the Pacific Ocean. Measured from its base on the seafloor to its peak, Mauna Kea is 31,796 feet (9,694 m) tall. All over the world, the oceans cover big sections of the tectonic plates, including almost all of the borders between them.

Where two tectonic plates come together, tremendous power is evident. Some plates slide along beside one another, forming earthquake zones such as California's famous San Andreas Fault. In many areas, plates meet head-on. In some cases, one plate will push the other one up and mountains are formed. In

Hawaii's Mauna Kea is seen rising into the distant clouds. It is the tallest mountain on Earth (measured from base to peak), but most of its height is below the waterline.

other cases, one will be crushed down into Earth's mantle while the other rides on top of it. These are called "subduction zones," and they correspond to the deep-ocean trenches. Narrow and crooked, they represent Earth's ultimate recycling plan. Entire continents are inexorably being driven back down, inch by inch, into the hot mantle. Deep below the crust of Earth, they will eventually be melted and become molten magma.

But perhaps the most amazing feature on our planet is a long line of sub-oceanic, rugged peaks that form along a major boundary between tectonic plates that are spreading apart. It is called the Mid-Ocean Ridge, and it can be traced, like the seam on a baseball, right around the planet, for 46,000 miles (74,000 km)—from the Atlantic, across the southern Pacific, and back up across the Arctic Ocean. It is most obvious from Iceland to Tristan de Cunha, near the southwest tip of Africa, where it stitches up the Atlantic Ocean. There is even a narrow canyon down the middle called a "rift valley." It is the very place where the world is being ripped open by the mantle pushing molten rock up from below. This is how and where Earth's crust is restored. As the magma oozes up from below, it solidifies into the longest mountain range on Earth, almost all of which is under-water. The material cools and becomes solid as it spreads out on either side of the rift valley. This means the Mid-Ocean Ridge is causing the seafloor to spread.

A cross-section of the North Atlantic Ocean basin, from the United States to Europe. The Mid-Atlantic Ridge contains the rift valley, where the plates are pulling apart and new crust is being formed by molten rock rising from the depths and spreading out along the ocean floor.

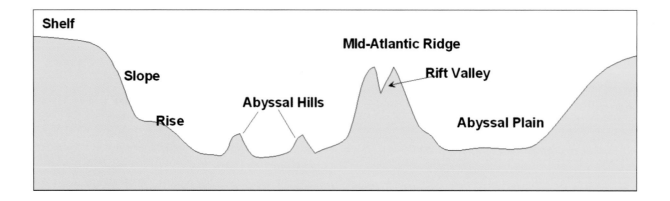

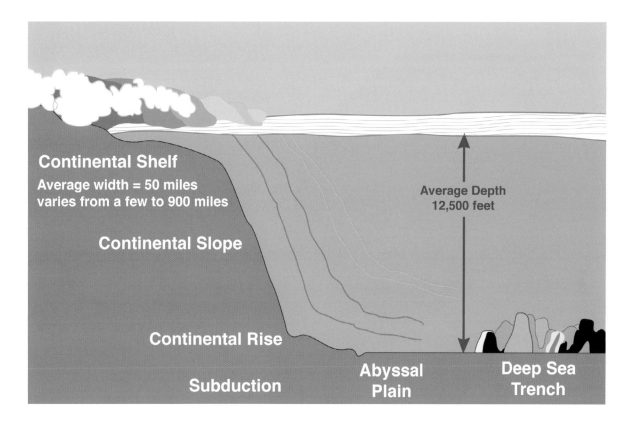

Continental Shelf
Average width = 50 miles
varies from a few to 900 miles

Continental Slope

Average Depth 12,500 feet

Continental Rise

Subduction

Abyssal Plain

Deep Sea Trench

Most of Earth's surface has been churned down into the mantle and then pushed back up more than once in the 4.6 billion years since the planet formed.

There are also many interesting features on the submerged parts of the plates. Each continent is rimmed with a shelf. The west coast of North America has a continental shelf that extends all the way from the farthest of the Aleutian Islands to the southern tip of Baja California. It is virtually unbroken except for narrow canyons. Extending out from the seashore just a few dozen miles, the continental shelf slopes rather gently downward. The depth of the continental shelf areas is mostly less than 1,000 feet (300 m). These areas are the great pastures of the sea, with vast quantities of tiny plants and animals. The floor of the continental shelf is rich with life because of the steady rain of nutrients from above.

This diagram shows a profile of the geography of the land as the edge of a continent meets the ocean. Every continental shelf drops first gradually and then dramatically to the ocean floor. The shallower waters above the continental shelves are teeming with ocean life.

In some places on the abyssal plain are dense fields of manganese nodules, such as this one, which was retrieved by an ROV.

If a person could walk out from the seashore onto the ocean floor, he or she would find that the continental shelf does not come to a sharp end, like the top of a cliff—at least not in most places around the world. Instead, the slope becomes gradually more pronounced. Within a few hundred steps, a person would definitely notice that he or she was headed downward at an angle comparable to a staircase. This steeper slope would take him or her far down to the level abyssal plains. Most of the ocean floor is one abyssal plain after another, interrupted by ranges of seamounts (underwater mountains) or long cracks called "fracture zones."

Many of the seamounts have flat tops; these are called "guyots" (GEE-oh). They were originally volcanic mountain peaks that rose above the surface and were worn down flat by the waves. Their enormous weight pressing down on the softer rock below caused them to gradually sink back underwater. Finally, there are the deep ocean trenches such as the Marianas Trench, the deepest spot in the world.

With fresh minerals steadily being exposed through seafloor spreading, the resource potential of the abyssal plains is enormous. Many of the abyssal plains are covered with mineral "nodules," fist-sized rocks with a high concentration of manganese and other important metals such as nickel. If the technology is ever developed that could retrieve the manganese nodules without ruining the environment of the ocean bottom, a tremendous bounty awaits.

Up the Food Chain

CHAPTER FIVE

Life needs energy. For all land animals—human beings included—the ultimate source of energy is the Sun. Sunlight shines down on plants, which use a molecule called chlorophyll to absorb the solar energy. This is the process of photosynthesis. Chemical reactions store the energy in the form of compounds that the plant needs for survival and growth. Glucose, for example, is a plant sugar that is based on six carbon atoms. When an animal eats green plants, the plants' energy gets converted into still more chemicals. Some of them are extremely complex. The list of animals that eat the other animals lower on the list for food is called the "food chain." At the bottom of the land-based food chain are green plants. Humans are at the very top of this food chain.

A humpback whale breaches, a common behavior that we still do not fully understand. These huge animals can consume many tons of tiny sea creatures each day. Whales are the top of the oceanic food chain.

In the upper layer of the oceans, life is magnificently abundant. The main difference between the food chain on land and that of the ocean is that in the seas there is no need for *roots*. At the bottom of the oceanic food chain are tiny life-forms called "plankton," which drift where the currents take them. They are mostly found within 1,000 feet (304 m) of the surface. Some plankton are plants, some are animals, and a few are curiously in between. Most consist of a single living cell.

Diatoms are the most basic plankton, and there are more than 15,000 different kinds of diatoms. Most are no bigger than one millimeter long; some are just one one-thousandth of that. Because of their small bodies, diatoms absorb nutrients from the seawater efficiently. They take in as much carbon dioxide and water molecules as their chlorophyll can process by photosynthesis, and pass oxygen gas back out to the ocean. When conditions are favorable, a new generation of diatoms grows in a mere eight hours. The sunlight falling on nine square feet (1 sq m) of the ocean surface provides energy for as many as eight billion diatoms.

It takes a stupendous number of living things at each step in the food chain to support the animals on the next step. Diatoms and other forms of plankton are the basic food for almost all life in the oceans. Many types of sharks, whales, and herrings are among the larger animals that eat them directly. A humpback whale can eat 400 billion diatoms in a few gulps, and it will be hungry again in a few hours. A baby blue whale gobbles up 6,000 pounds (2,700 kg) of tiny, shrimp-like animals called krill in a single day, and gains 90 pounds (40 kg) as a result. Scientists estimate that, of every 10 million living things in the ocean, only one dies of old age. The rest are eaten by animals higher up in the food chain, including people. The United States government has reported that the average American eats about 15 pounds (6.5 kg) of fish and shellfish each year. And there are almost 300 million Americans. For the entire world population, seafood provides about five percent of our total proteins, which are important chemicals in the human diet.

What sort of food is available for life processes deeper in the ocean, below the depth at which plankton thrive? Because of the blanketing darkness, almost all

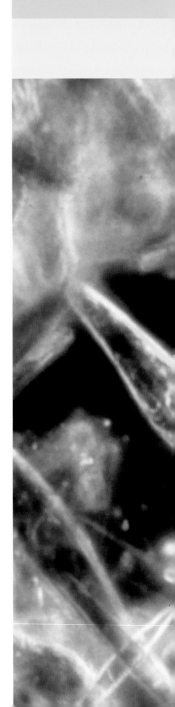

A variety of tiny marine diatoms as seen through a microscope. They form the bottom of the oceanic food chain. These creatures have a hard shell, called an exoskeleton, composed of silica—the same substance of which sand is formed.

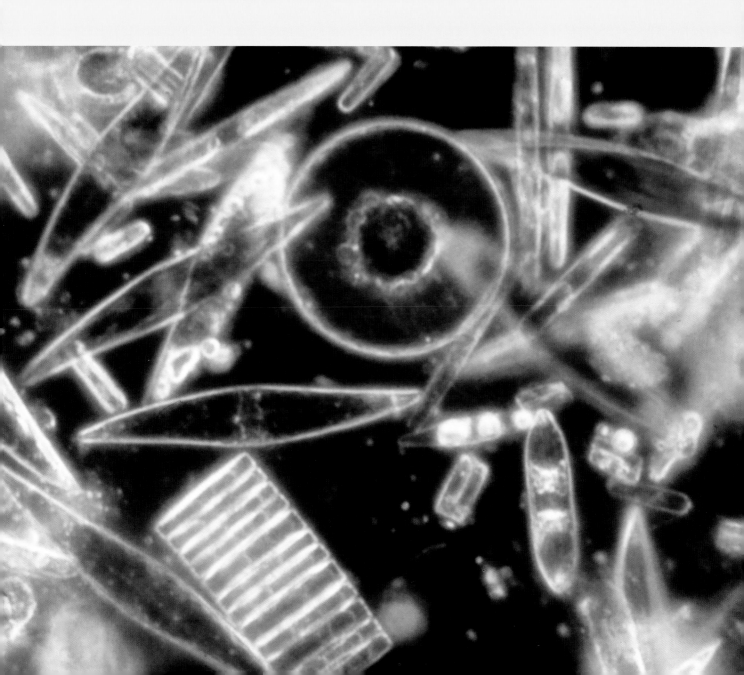

nutrition inevitably comes from above: plants and animals of all shapes and sizes sink down to the seafloor, usually after they are dead. There are also a great variety of bacteria that feed on the once-living matter and break down the chemicals that other creatures can use as food. The bacteria are single-celled creatures even simpler than diatoms. They are not much more than tiny chemical factories, but scientists have found bacteria in every corner of the world—even 1,300 feet (400 m) beneath the ocean floor!

Some animals, such as sea cucumbers, move slowly through the ooze at the bottom of the ocean. They swallow the mud as they move, digesting anything that might be nutritious. Sea cucumbers are examples of "infauna"—creatures that live partly or entirely underground at the bottom of the sea. Animals that are found on the bottom itself are called "epifauna." One group that falls into this category are starfishes. Although starfishes have a familiar and more attractive appearance than many deep-sea beasts, they are efficient predators that eat clams and other shellfish. One way or another, every living thing must process energy to survive.

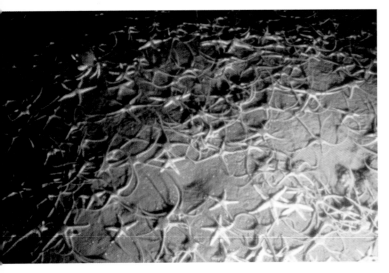

Top: Strange creatures abound on the ocean floor, such as this sea cucumber. The photographer placed a diver's knife next to it to give a sense of scale. This sea cucumber is more than a foot (.3 m) long.

Bottom: Many types of starfish are also found in the black depths of the ocean floor, such as these brittle stars. Outside of the field of the camera's light it is utterly dark.

Beyond the Aquarium

The simplest living things in the oceans, such as diatoms, are separated into categories by how they survive: Plants get energy from the Sun, while animals eat things. Larger and more complicated animals can be distinguished by how they move or hold themselves up.

"Invertebrates" are animals that have hardly any bones at all and are almost shapeless. This category includes jellyfish. Some species float on the surface and have dangerous stingers, such as the pale blue or pink Portuguese man-of-war, which is actually a colony of separate animals growing together. In deep water there are jellyfish with more vivid colors and swirling shapes that look somewhat like hats and saucers.

With about 200 slime glands all over its body, the hagfish could win the title of most unappealing invertebrate. Long and eel-shaped, hagfish attack and eat smaller fish, or they scavenge food from dead creatures lying on the ocean bottom. Hagfish are blind, jawless, and finless, yet their skin can be tanned and turned into a valuable substitute for leather.

An octopus is also an invertebrate, as is a squid. With peculiarly shaped bodies, sucker cups on their arms and tentacles, and jet-powered movement, it is impossible to imagine them anywhere but in the ocean. Both have highly developed eyes and a hard, parrot-like beak. The largest of them is the giant squid, which has starred in many science-fiction stories and may even be the cause of "sea monster" stories that were told by sailors during the Age of Exploration. Dead ones turn up often on beaches from New England to New Zealand, and they can be 60 feet (18 m) long, with suckers the size of cereal bowls. Giant squid remain mysterious—no one has ever managed to photograph a live one moving in the ocean.

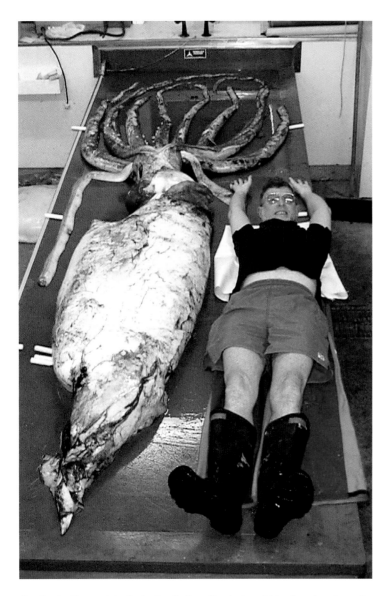

A scientist lies next to the body of a juvenile giant squid to show how large it is. An adult giant squid may reach well over 100 feet (30 m) in length. A live giant squid has never been caught.

The largest group of swimming animals is fish, but the category is sub-divided according to the kind of skeleton they have. Sharks and rays are species that have skeletons made out of cartilage, which is softer and more flexible than bones. Feared because of their ferocious attacks, sharks have several rows of teeth—if a shark loses a tooth, another one swings down from its jaw, ready for the next meal. There are at least 350 separate species of sharks, and some have been seen more than 6,500 feet (2,000 m) below the surface of the sea.

Most fish species have solid bones like ours. Some are adapted for fast swimming, others for long-distance cruising, and still others for nimble maneuvers. In the dark depths, extremely unusual fish species abound. Although it's only about 10 inches (25 cm) long, the nasty viperfish has long, needle-sharp teeth. It can extend its oversized lower jaw downward and bend its upper jaw backward to gobble up prey larger than itself. Viperfish come up to a depth of 200 feet (60 m) at night, but they spend the daytime hours almost 10,000 feet (3,000 m) down.

Another mini-monster is the grotesque anglerfish. Pear-shaped and up to a yard (1 m) long, a female anglerfish has a menacing appearance. From her forehead, a long lure extends forward in front of her mouth. At the end of the lure is an organ that glows like a feeble lamp, which attracts other fish. If they are curious enough to get too close, the anglerfish will dart forward and attack, often swallowing the prey whole.

The light at the end of the anglerfish's lure is an example of "bioluminescence": light energy created by a living thing. Many deep-ocean fishes have a pattern of "photophores," or light-emitting cells, all over their skins. The light is emitted by a chemical called luciferin. Scientists think bioluminescence helps the fish in a variety of ways. The pattern of lights could attract a mate, or perhaps a meal. It might be a form of camouflage, making other predators think something larger is lurking there. It is even possible that it is a signal to other fish of the same species, so that they can attack in a group. One thing is certain: in the deep ocean, the soft glow of the bioluminescent fish is absolutely the only light in the black darkness.

One of the nastiest-looking, and deadliest, of the creatures of the deep is the viperfish, which has fangs so long that they do not fit into the animal's jaws.

Whales and dolphins are not fish at all, and they have complete skeletons like human beings have. They are mammals, and their history goes back millions of years to a time when their ancestors lived on land. Why whales and dolphins returned to the sea so many generations in the past is not known, but some of them now swim deep into the ocean, perhaps as deep as 10,000 feet (3,000 m). A sperm whale can be up to 60 feet (18 m) long and remain underwater without breathing for 90 minutes! Sperm whales eat squid and are often found with marks on their skin caused by the suckers of a giant squid as it tried to defend itself from a whale's attack. Another feature of the sperm whale is the

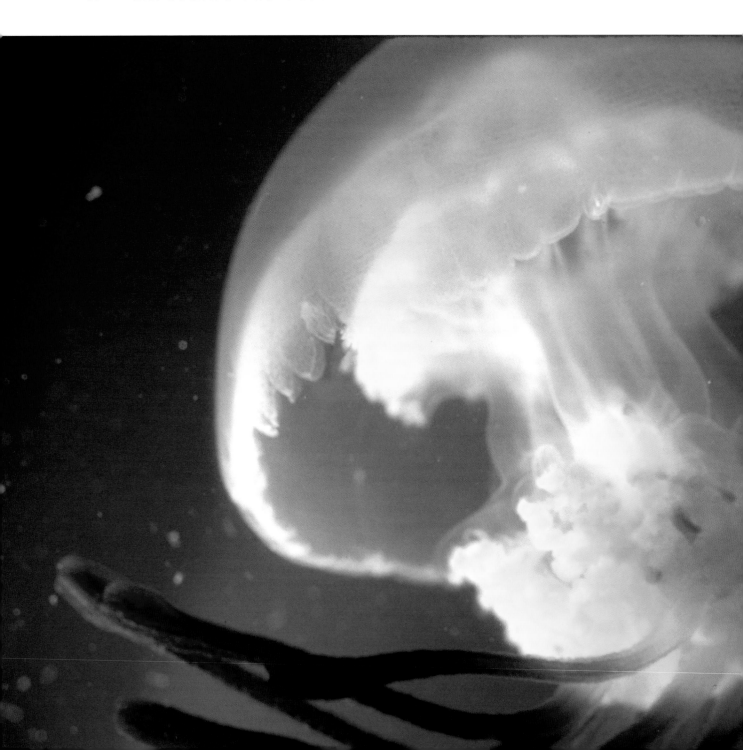

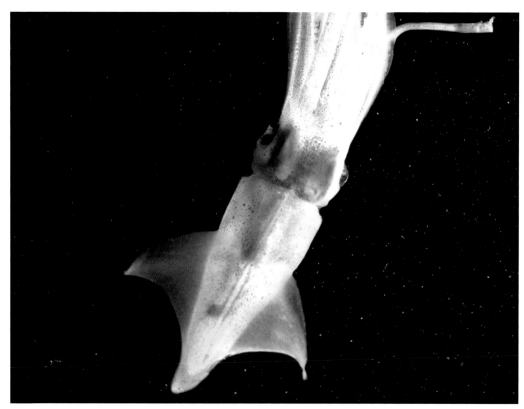

huge amount of oil, called "spermaceti," held in chambers in its skull. Scientists think the whale uses the spermaceti—as much as 1,000 gallons (4,200 l) of it—to amplify the noises it makes. And spermaceti may also help the whale float. But for centuries, the oil was prized by human beings for burning in lamps. As a result, sperm whales were mercilessly hunted until just a few years ago.

Left: One example of marine bioluminescence is this jellyfish, lit from the inside.

Above: Another bioluminescent sea creature is the squid. Not all squid have this ability. Bioluminescence is found mostly in those that live at great depths.

At the Very Bottom

CHAPTER SEVEN

To study the unexplored territory at the bottom of the ocean, *Alvin* made many dives to the Mid-Ocean Ridge in the 1970s. On one expedition, Robert Ballard and the scientists with him saw deep-sea vents for the first time. As they watched, fountains of hot, dirty water came spewing out of cracks in the rock. Nudging closer, they extended a thermometer out from *Alvin* on a robotic arm. The reading went off the scale, and then the thermometer melted. Also called "hydrothermal" (hot water) vents, these gushing fissures surprised the scientists who thought the bottom of the ocean was a peaceful place. The use of deep-diving ROVs has helped to map fields of hydrothermal vents on the seafloor all over the world, most of them near the Mid-Ocean Ridge or similar features.

Because the hot water exiting the vents is forced out under tremendous pressure, its temperature is well above the boiling point of water and has been measured as high as 750°F (400°C). There are a few places on land where something quite similar happens, such as the famous Old Faithful geyser in Yellowstone Park. The cause of the heat and pressure is the same partly molten rock mantle that lies under all the tectonic plates and forces the seafloor to spread apart at the Mid-Ocean Ridge. (In Yellowstone, the heat and pressure superheats underground water and forces it back up through the crust.) Scientists calculate that every drop of water in the entire world is circulated under the ocean floor every six to eight million years.

Old Faithful erupts through a process quite similar to that which powers the hydrothermal vents found near the Mid-Ocean Ridge.

Under the oceans, Earth's crust is not nearly as thick as the exposed landmasses, averaging only about three miles (5 km) deep. Coming from an inferno of flowing rock, up through this cracked layer, the water is a rich brew of dissolved chemicals. Some of the chemicals are noxious poisons, such as sulfur and hydrogen sulfide. Hydrogen sulfide is a well-known compound because of its characteristic smell of rotten eggs.

Also coming out are metal elements, and the hydrothermal vents are probably the chief source of the minerals that form the manganese nodules found all over the seafloor. As the hot water rushes from the vents into the cold water of the ocean, some material crystallizes into rock columns dozens of feet tall. These features in the deep ocean are called "black smoker chimneys."

A black smoker chimney on the bottom of the ocean. The dark, dissolved poisonous chemicals that spew forth from the smoker can be hotter than 750°F (398°C). And yet, a thriving community of strange animals is found around each one of the smoker chimneys.

A remote-controlled arm from *Alvin* breaks off a piece of a black smoker chimney to bring back to the surface for study.

They grow rapidly. *Alvin* broke one off by accident in 1993, and when scientists returned only three months later, the chimney was 20 feet (6 m) taller!

No sunlight penetrates down to the deep ocean, so scientists had expected to find no interesting life-forms at the very bottom. Yet they saw large numbers of recognizable creatures such as worms, clams, crabs, shrimps, and even octopi. These animals were pale in color and most had either no eyes or eyes that were obviously very different from their surface-dwelling counterparts. Biologist Cindy Van Dover investigated the way some of these creatures' eyes might work. Her team photographed the hydrothermal vents with cameras that are extremely sensitive to the slightest source of light. She was astounded to learn that there was a dim but noticeable glow coming from the hot vent water itself. Too dim to be noticed by humans, the glow is sufficient for those creatures near the vents to see.

Bottom dwellers do not benefit from photosynthesis, since no sunlight is present. Where, then, do they get the energy to live? The answer is that there are microscopic bacteria able to eat the hydrogen sulfide spurting out of the hydrothermal vents. Instead of photosynthesis, these basic life-forms concentrate energy by a process called "chemosynthesis." The hydrogen sulfide is like sunlight to them. Through chemosynthesis, the bacteria convert hydrogen sulfide, oxygen, and carbon dioxide into types of sugars.

The animals on the ocean bottom do not just gobble up and digest the bacteria. The stomachs of some clam and shrimp species surrounding the hydrothermal vents are filled with *living* bacteria, too. Each species needs the other for survival, an example of what biologists call "mutual symbiosis."

In 1977, Ballard and three colleagues made the strangest discovery of all, peering out *Alvin's* windows. Next to a hydrothermal vent, in the dark, hot, poisonous water, they saw tube worms attached to the rocks. A different life-form from any that exists on land, tube worms range up to about six feet (1.8 m) in height and are typically an inch or so (2.5 cm) wide. They cluster together in large numbers. The white tubes, with something like a collar at the top, are made by the tube worms themselves. Each tube worm has a plume—a bright red tip that it waves out the top of its tube. The worms' white, tubular homes are made of a tough, natural material called chitin, the same substance from which lobster shells are formed.

Tube worms have no mouths nor stomachs. Their blood is rich in hemoglobin, the same chemical that carries oxygen in human blood. But in the tube worm, the blood absorbs hydrogen sulfide from the water around the tube worm's plume. Then the blood carries the noxious chemical down into the tube worm's body—which is stuffed full of billions of sulfur-loving bacteria. In an arrangement that benefits both, the microscopic bacteria accept the chemicals, and the tube worm gets sugars and other life-giving chemicals in return.

This tube worm colony is so thick that you cannot see the black smoker chimney to which it is attached. The worms, when stretched out, can be more than 10 feet (3 m) long.

Cold Seeps

"Cold seeps" are places where high-pressure bubbles of methane gas come up from below the sea floor through ice crystals made of "methane hydrate." Methane is a promising energy source for the future, and dozens of cold seeps have now been found around the world. Chuck Fisher, a biologist from Penn State University, discovered "ice worms," less than 2 inches (4 cm) in length, crawling around on the methane hydrate. Scientists suspect these ice worms eat bacteria that get energy from the methane by chemosynthesis.

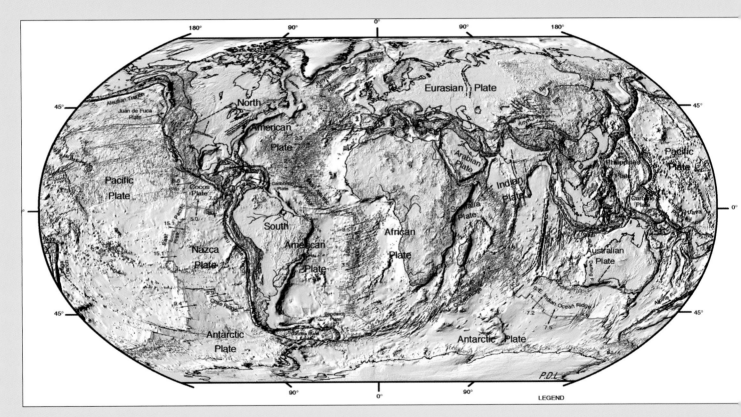

With the oceans removed, the edges and shapes of the planet's tectonic plates are revealed. Where the edges of two plates meet, there is an indication of the speed at which they are spreading apart from each other at that point, listed in centimeters. Cold seeps are generally found right off the continental shelves, although some are also found at the edges of the plates. The red dots indicate areas of volcanic activity over the past one million years.

Living in the Sea

CHAPTER EIGHT

When astronauts are launched toward the International Space Station, people can watch them on television. But there are usually four or five "aquanauts" who are never seen on TV, on board a different kind of space station named *Aquarius*. It's 47 feet (14 m) beneath the surface of the Atlantic Ocean off Key Largo, Florida. The surroundings are beautiful coral reefs and a myriad of shallow-water fishes. Although they enjoy the views, the occupants are not on vacation. They are scientists and technicians, hard at work observing the environment.

Aquarius is a research station and the only permanent undersea habitat in the world. It's as close as human beings have yet come to building the undersea city that has been a dream for centuries. A base weighing 116 tons (105 t) holds the 43-foot-long (13 m), 9-foot-wide (2.7 m) steel research station fast on the seafloor. Like a well-equipped motor home, it has bunks for six scientists, along with a kitchen, washroom facilities, and a workroom.

Marine biologists who want to study the local aquatic plant and animal life can take advantage of the facility for missions that usually last 10 days. If they wanted to dive down from the surface every day to work, they would need to spend many hours on the way down and many more on the way back up to clear the nitrogen molecules from their blood; otherwise, nitrogen bubbles could form in their bodies, a dangerous condition divers call "the bends." But from the underwater base, biologists can slip into the ocean whenever they need to and go to work immediately without having to worry about the bends.

Would someone *want* to spend his or her whole life at the bottom of the sea? French architect Jacques Rougerie designed a practical village that could be a home on the ocean floor. Rougerie built smaller habitats in the 1970s and 1980s,

A cutaway view of the interior of the *Aquarius* shows research areas and living quarters for four scientists.

including "Aquabubbles" that could be moved from one place to another when required. But his dream is bigger: aquatic villages that would each be home to about 2,500 people.

The inhabitants would live in domed houses with doorways on the underside so they could enter and exit more easily. They would swim to other domes where crops such as kelp would be grown, or pens where they would raise fish for food. There would be workshops, stores, and community buildings, and the whole town would be anchored at a reasonably shallow location on the continental shelf. Rougerie envisions a network of such villages all over the oceans.

There were many experiments in the 1960s to prove that human beings could live, for a few weeks at least, in ocean habitats. French oceanographer Jacques Cousteau built a series of structures called "Conshelf," named for the continental shelf. The U.S. Navy commissioned three habitats, each named *SeaLab*, where Navy divers lived and conducted research for weeks at a time. The Navy was acutely interested in life aboard military submarines, and in 1960, the nuclear-

Opposite page: The undersea habitat *Aquarius* is ready to be shipped to its drop point off the Florida coast in 1986.

In the 1960s, Jacques Cousteau's *Conshelf II* was home to five scientists for a period of one month. It is now abandoned and overgrown.

powered *USS Triton* became the first vessel to travel around the world completely underwater. Since then, Navy submarine missions are routinely scheduled to last for many months.

Robert Ballard has proposed that living in the sea should take place right at the surface. He developed a design for a long, narrow, floating structure that would be built at a dockyard, then towed out to sea and tipped so that it was vertical. The part above the water would be as comfortable and luxurious as an apartment building or hotel. The lower section, reaching a few hundred feet (100 m) down, would house machinery to generate electricity from the difference in temperature between the surface layer and the deep, cold water.

Getting around under the sea will be a lot easier if diver Graham Hawkes succeeds in building *Deep Flight Aviator*, a two-person submersible the size and shape of a small airplane. Much less expensive than taking a dive in a research submersible such as *Alvin* or *Shinkai*, *Deep Flight Aviator* could make it possible for many non-scientists to enjoy a quick visit to the wonders of the sea. A special diving license would be needed to "fly" it.

None of these projects involve putting civilization at the bottom of the deep ocean. The incredible pressure and the darkness make it difficult to imagine how a large community could live there. But shallower areas, such as the continental shelves, may one day become home to small communities of adventurous people around the world. Now that we have people routinely living in orbit around Earth, the ocean depths remain as the final frontier for human exploration.

Visit a Sea Habitat

The *Ben Franklin* was built in Switzerland and submerged off the coast of Florida in 1969. With a crew of six, the 50-foot (15 m) submersible drifted in the Gulf Stream at a depth of 1,000 feet (300 m) for four weeks. After a voyage of 1,400 miles (2,250 km), the *Ben Franklin* was hoisted back to the surface off the coast of Maine. The experimental habitat was bought by John Horton, an oil-exploration businessman, in the 1970s. Horton wanted to use the *Ben Franklin* to hunt for drilling sites under the ice in the Arctic, but that never happened, and the vessel sat at a dockyard in Vancouver, Canada. In 2002, Horton donated the *Ben Franklin* to the Vancouver Maritime Museum, and the staff has refurbished it for visitors to look at.

The *Ben Franklin* submersible, built by Auguste Piccard, who pioneered the development of the bathyscaphe. Below is a cutaway view of the interior.

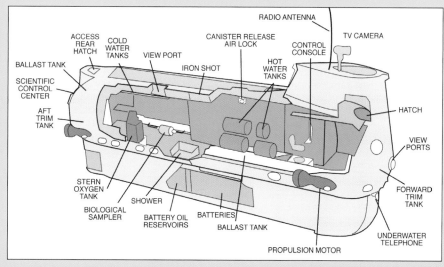

abyssal zone The vast deep areas of the ocean; also called the abyss.

aquabubble Movable habitat intended for use as a home on the ocean floor.

aquanaut One who lives and works both inside and outside an underwater shelter.

atom The smallest particle of an element that can exist alone or in combination.

AUV An autonomous underwater vehicle not connected to a ship on the surface by cable.

bathyscaph A submersible vessel for deep-sea exploration capable of being controlled by its crew.

bathysphere The first apparatus designed to send a human being deep into the ocean.

benthic zone An area near the bottom of the ocean, whether under deep or shallow water.

bioluminescence Light energy emitted by a living organism.

black smoker chimney Rock column that forms when hot water from a hydrothermal vent mixes with cold ocean water.

cartilage Material that makes up the skeleton of certain animals. It is softer and more flexible than bone.

chemosynthesis A process by which certain microscopic bacteria convert hydrogen sulfide and other compounds into sugars.

continental shelf The relatively shallow area that lies around each major landmass on Earth.

diatom The most basic plankton.

epifauna Animals that live on the ocean bottom.

fracture zone A long crack or rupture in an abyssal plain.

guyot The flat top of a seamount.

hadal zone The very deepest individual places in the ocean.

hydrophone Underwater microphone for the detection of sound waves.

hydrothermal vent Fountain of extremely hot water gushing from fissures in the ocean floor.

infauna Creatures that live partly or entirely underground at the ocean bottom.

invertebrates Category of animals that lack a spinal column.

krill Tiny shrimp-like animals.

mantle The main body of Earth.

molecule The smallest particle of a substance that keeps the properties of the substance and is made up of one or more atoms.

pelagic zone All of the ocean water.

photophores Light-emitting cells on the skin of many deep-ocean fishes.

photosynthesis Process by which energy from the Sun is converted to chemical compounds needed by plants for survival and growth. Especially important in this process is a plant molecule known as chlorophyll.

plankton Minute life-forms that comprise the bottom of the food chain in the oceans. Plankton may be plants or animals, and a few have characteristics of both.

rift valley An elongated, narrow valley where Earth's crust bursts open, pushing molten rock up from the mantle.

ROV A remotely operated vehicle for underwater exploration. It is usually controlled from the surface.

salinity Amount of saltiness of (ocean) water.

seamount A submarine mountain that rises from an abyssal plain.

spermaceti The oil held in an organ in the skull of a sperm whale.

subduction zone The area where two tectonic plates meet head-on, causing one plate to be crushed down into Earth's mantle while the other plate rides on top.

submersible An undersea vessel that operates solely below the surface.

symbiosis The living together of two dissimilar organisms that benefits both.

tectonic plate An enormous piece of Earth's outer crust that slides over the mantle.

telepresence Transmission of discoveries by live signal from the operators of an undersea robot to a distant audience.